Comptroller of the Currency
Administrator of National Banks

Retail Nondeposit Investment Sales

Comptroller's Handbook
(Section 413)

February 1994

Other Income Producing Activities

Retail Nondeposit Investment Sales (Section 413)

Table of Contents

This section sets forth guidance for examiners reviewing bank nondeposit investment product retail sales operations, including bank-related marketing and promotional activities. Examiners will review a bank's programs for consistency with the Interagency Statement on Retail Sales of Nondeposit Investment Products, dated February 15, 1994 (interagency Statement). The evaluation will cover all bank-related activities including:

- Sales or recommendations made by bank employees;
- Sales or recommendations made by employees of affiliated or unaffiliated entities occurring on bank premises (including sales or recommendations initiated by telephone or by mail from bank premises); and
- Sales resulting from referrals of retail customers to a third party when the bank receives a benefit for the referral.

When reviewing a bank's nondeposit investment sales operation, examiners should determine that the bank views customers' interests as critical to all aspects of its sales programs. Examiners should evaluate a bank's policies and procedures from the customers' perspective and should ascertain that customers are provided with a high level of protection. If it becomes necessary to recommend remedial action, examiners should determine that bank management responds immediately to any matter that has the potential to confuse customers as to the uninsured nature of nondeposit investment products.

Banks that do not operate programs safely and soundly or that engage in violations of law or regulations will be subject to appropriate regulatory action. When determining the appropriate action, examiners should be mindful that some banks, especially banks relying on third parties for sales of nondeposit investment products, may need time to conform their programs to the Interagency Statement and to the guidance contained herein. At a minimum, however, examiners should determine whether bank management is making a good faith effort to comply with this regulatory guidance in a timely manner.

This section applies to sales to individual customers but does not apply to the wholesale sale of nondeposit investment products to non-retail customers, such as sales to institutional customers or to fiduciary accounts administered by an institution. As part of its general responsibilities, however, a national bank should take appropriate steps to avoid potential customer confusion when providing nondeposit investment products to institutional customers or to the bank's fiduciary customers. For additional information on restrictions on a national bank's use as fiduciary of the bank's brokerage service or other entity with which the bank has a conflict of interest, including purchases of the bank's proprietary and other products, see 12 CFR 9.12 and "Sales to Fiduciary Accounts," later in this section.

Scope

Examiner reviews of a bank's mutual fund or other nondeposit investment sales program will concentrate on the policies and procedures the bank adopts and on the effectiveness of their implementation.

When reviewing implementation of a bank's program, examiners will investigate whether senior bank management has:

(1) Participated in planning the bank's investment sales program;
(2) Adopted a framework to ensure compliance with all applicable laws, rules, regulations, regulatory conditions, and the Interagency Statement; and
(3) Ensured effective supervision of individuals engaged in sales activities, including employees of the bank and any other entity involved in bank-related sales of investment products.

Where relevant, references in this handbook section to bank management or bank employees includes third party managers or third party employees.

Minimum Standards for Nondeposit Investment Programs

Antifraud provisions of the federal securities laws prohibit materially misleading or inaccurate representation in connection with offers and sales of securities. (See, for example, Section 10 of the Securities Exchange Act of 1934 and Rule 10b-5.) If customers are misled about the nature of nondeposit investment products, including their uninsured status, sellers could face potential liability under these antifraud provisions. Safe and sound banking also requires that bank-related retail sales activities be operated to avoid confusing customers about the products being offered. Use of nonbank employees to sell these products does not relieve bank management of the responsibility to take reasonable steps to ensure that the investment sales activities meet these requirements.

The Rules of Fair Practice of the National Association of Securities Dealers (NASD) expressly govern sales of securities by broker/dealers who are members of NASD. These rules apply to bank-related securities sales by banking subsidiaries registered as broker/dealers, affiliated broker/dealers, and unaffiliated broker/dealers operating under agreements with banks. These rules apply whether such sales are made on bank premises or at a separate location.

These rules do not expressly apply to sales or recommendations made directly by the bank. Even when these rules do not expressly apply, however, they are an appropriate reference for a bank compliance program designed to ensure that the bank's retail sales of all nondeposit investment products are operated in a safe and sound manner.

Before beginning to operate a nondeposit investment sales program, banks may also consider notifying their blanket bond carriers of plans to engage in these activities. If applicable, this could permit the bank to obtain written assurances from the carrier that the bank's insurance coverage for employees includes staff representing third party vendors.

Examiners also should encourage bank management to review Retail Investment Sales: Guidelines for Banks. The publication, prepared jointly by six banking industry trade associations, contains voluntary guidelines for bank sales of nondeposit investment products as well as common sense suggestions for putting many of the OCC's recommendations into action.

Program Management

Banks must comply with all applicable laws, rules, regulations, and regulatory conditions, and operate consistently with the Interagency Statement for any of their bank-related retail sales of mutual funds, annuities, or other retail nondeposit investment products. Bank directors are responsible for evaluating the risks imposed by bank-related sales and are expected to adopt a program statement and self-regulatory policies and procedures to ensure compliance with all requirements. A bank's policies and procedures must address bank-related retail sales made directly by a bank, through an operating subsidiary or affiliate, or by an unaffiliated entity.

Examiners should expect that banks will tailor their policies and procedures to the scope of the bank's sales activities. The level of detail contained in a bank's policies and procedures will depend on the structure and complexity of the bank's program.

Examiners will review the bank's securities sales activities to determine that the bank has adopted a statement that addresses the risks associated with the sales program and describes the features of the sales program, the roles of bank employees, and the roles of third party entities. The statement should set forth the strategies the bank will employ to achieve its objectives. It also should outline the self-regulatory procedures bank management will implement to ensure that the program's objectives are met without compromising the customers' best interests.

At a minimum, examiners should expect bank policies and procedures to address:

Supervision of personnel involved in nondeposit investment sales programs — Senior bank managers will be expected to ensure that specific individuals employed by the bank, an affiliated broker/dealer, or a third party vendor are responsible for each activity outlined in the bank's policies and procedures. Managers of the bank's securities sales activities will be accountable for understanding the investment products offered and the sales process, as well as for assuring compliance with securities and banking laws, rules, and regulations.

Designation of employees authorized to sell investment products — This should serve as a guide for all bank-related employees dealing with retail nondeposit investment product customers. The program statement should specify that only properly trained and supervised employees are permitted to make investment sales or recommendations. It should describe the responsibilities of personnel authorized to sell or recommend nondeposit investment products and of other personnel who may have contact with retail customers concerning the sales program. It also should include a description of appropriate and inappropriate referral activities and the training requirements and compensation arrangements for each category of personnel.

The roles of other entities selling on bank premises, including supervision of selling employees — Bank management must plan to monitor compliance by other entities on an ongoing basis. The degree of bank management's involvement should be dictated by the nature and extent of nondeposit investment product sales, the effectiveness of customer protection systems, and customer responses. (See "Third Party Vendors," later in this section for more details on programs operated by third parties.)

The types of products sold — Policies and procedures should include the criteria the bank will use to select and review each type of product sold or recommended.

For each type of product sold by bank employees, the bank should identify specific laws, regulations, regulatory conditions, and any other limitation or requirements, including qualitative considerations, that will expressly govern the selection and marketing of products the bank will offer. (See "Product Selection," later in this section for further discussion of these issues.)

Examiners should review:

- The process the bank uses to select the products it will offer,
- What the bank did to ensure the products meet its customers' needs and expectations, and
- How well the bank is performing an ongoing analysis of the appropriateness of the products offered for sale.

Examiners will also assess the independence and thoroughness of the analysis and the degree to which the bank relies on ratings services. Examiners should be critical of bank managers who simply choose products that generate the largest sales fees or accept what a third party has to offer without performing an independent analysis of the suitability of the products to the bank's strategy and customer mix.

Examiners should not give the impression that the agency expects bank managers to be "stock pickers" or that it intends to expand or limit the types of products banks offer. Instead, examiners should determine that bankers are selecting products that generally meet their customers' needs.

(See "Third Party Vendors," later in this section, for more details on the bank's oversight roles when it relies on its third party vendor to select products.)

Policies governing the permissible uses of bank customer information — Examiners should determine that bank customer information policies address the permissible uses of such information for any purpose associated with bank-related retail investment sales activity. In particular, if the bank intends to use customer lists to telephone depositors whose certificates of deposit are due to mature to inform them about alternative investment products, the policies should outline steps the bank will take to avoid confusing customers as to the risks associated with nondeposit investment products, including their uninsured nature.

Banks may also supply customer information lists to a third party vendor. Supplying such information should only occur, however, after bank management has evaluated steps the third party is taking to avoid confusing customers and after determining such steps are consistent with bank policy.

Bank management also may wish to consider obtaining a legal opinion concerning the bank's authority to share customer information with third parties.

Communications with customers — Examiners should determine whether the bank's policies consider the need for periodic and ongoing communications with customers to help them understand their investments and to remind customers periodically that the products they have purchased are not insured deposits. Policies should outline customer communications for the bank during periods of market stress and assign responsibilities for such communications.

Setting and Circumstances of Nondeposit Investment Product Sales

Banks should market nondeposit products in a manner that does not mislead or confuse customers as to the nature of the products or their risks. The setting and circumstances surrounding sales of investment products is fundamental to ensuring that customers can readily distinguish between nondeposit investment products and insured deposits. Examiners will determine that bank management has established controls to distinguish retail deposit-taking activities from the promotion, sale, and subsequent customer relationships related to retail nondeposit investment sales.

To minimize customer confusion, sales of, or recommendations for, nondeposit investment products on the bank's premises should be conducted in a physical location distinct from the area where retail deposits are taken. Signs or other means should be used to distinguish the investment sales area from the retail deposit-taking area of the institution.

In the limited situation in which physical considerations prevent nondeposit investment product operations from being conducted in a distinct area of the bank, a bank has a heightened responsibility to ensure that measures are in place to minimize customer confusion. To minimize customer confusion, the bank should make an officer responsible for each of the locations at which the investment product sales will take place.

The bank also should employ signs and, where possible, separate desks and personnel for deposit-taking and investment product sales. Investment product salespeople should clearly identify themselves by the use of appropriate methods such as name tags or separate business cards. In banks where the investment program is likely to be less elaborate, the examiner should determine, at a minimum, that the bank utilizes the written and oral disclosures described below.

In no case should any employee, while located in the routine deposit-taking area, such as the teller window, make general or specific investment recommendations regarding nondeposit investment products, or accept orders for such products, even if unsolicited. Tellers and other employees who are not authorized to sell nondeposit investment products may only refer customers to individuals who are specifically designated and trained to assist customers interested in the purchase of such products.

Product names — Banks may not offer nondeposit investment products with a product name identical to the bank's name. Names that imply that mutual funds are U.S. government guaranteed also are prohibited.

Banks also should recognize that the potential for customer confusion may be increased if the bank offers nondeposit product names that are similar to the bank's name. If the bank offers such nondeposit products with names similar to the bank's, it should design sales training programs to minimize the risk of confusing customers.

In addition, Securities and Exchange Commission (SEC) staff have issued an opinion that common names between a bank and a mutual fund sold or marketed by or through that bank are presumed to be misleading and a violation of the Investment Company Act of 1940. SEC staff contends, however, that a common name fund can rebut the presumption that a fund's name is misleading by ensuring that the cover page of the prospectus prominently discloses that the fund's shares are not deposits or obligations of the bank and are not federally insured.

When examining investment sales programs in a bank that is selling funds with names similar to the bank's, examiners will evaluate the steps that bank management has taken to avoid confusing customers. The greater the similarity between bank and fund names, the more closely examiners will scrutinize all aspects of a bank's sales program.

Examiners should criticize sales programs in which fund names are so similar to the bank's that even mitigating circumstances are unlikely to eliminate customer confusion. For example, it may be acceptable for "First National Bank" to offer a nondeposit investment product named "First Fund" as long as the bank has implemented sufficient disclosures, training, and other measures to mitigate customer confusion. Other names, however, such as "First Bank Fund" or "First National Fund" are so similar to a bank's name that they are inappropriate because they are inherently confusing.

Examiners and bank management should also be aware that the potential for customer confusion can depend on the context in which the sales are taking place. For example, it may be inappropriate for the First National Bank to offer a mutual fund product named "FNB Money Market Fund" if First National Bank were also offering an insured deposit product named "FNB Money Market Account."

Overall setting and circumstances — When reviewing nondeposit investment product sales operations, examiners should not place undue weight on a single aspect of the setting and circumstances of the sale. Each bank's sales program is different, and one set of rules may not cover all circumstances or provide all customers with the necessary level of protection. Before judging a particular bank's operations, examiners should consider how the various elements of the program interact and whether the elements combined mislead or avoid misleading customers.

The following example illustrates how the combination of certain elements can potentially mislead customers:

> An employee of the First National Bank sits at a desk in the lobby. This employee sells money market mutual funds and renews CDs. The employee tells customers about two products the bank is offering: the FNB Money Market Fund, an uninsured retail nondeposit investment product, and the FNB Money Market Account, an insured deposit. This employee may have an incentive to market the uninsured product because the employee gets a commission for selling a mutual fund but receives nothing for selling or renewing a deposit.

This situation could confuse customers. To mitigate customer confusion, the bank should ensure that the employee has extensive knowledge of the products being sold and that the employee is thoroughly aware of customer protection issues. When selling noninsured products, the employee should also require customers to sign a new account form acknowledging that the product is not insured.

If space and personnel limitations appear to increase the potential for customer confusion, examiners should encourage bank management to require additional training and disclosures, develop signs and product names that clearly distinguish among the products being sold, and assure that compensation for selling uninsured and insured products is equalized. Examiners should expect banks with nondeposit investment sales programs already in operation when this section is issued to initiate actions immediately to conform all aspects of the setting and circumstances of the bank's program to these requirements. In particular, banks should take immediate steps to correct any elements that could confuse customers.

Disclosures and Advertising

Disclosures

Complete and accurate disclosure must be provided to avoid customer confusion as to whether a bank-related product is an investment product or an insured bank deposit. Examiners should determine that banks selling, advertising, or otherwise marketing nondeposit investment products to retail customers provide the following product disclosures conspicuously: The products offered (1) are not FDIC insured, (2) are not deposits or other obligations of the bank or guaranteed by the bank, and (3) involve investment risks, including possible loss of principal amount invested.

The minimum disclosures should be provided to the customer:

- Orally during any sales presentation.
- Orally when investment advice concerning nondeposit investment products is provided.
- Orally and in writing prior to or at the time an investment account is opened to purchase these products.
- In advertisements and other promotional materials, as described below.

Examiners will determine whether these disclosures are featured conspicuously in all written or oral sales presentations, advertising and promotional materials, prospectuses, confirmations, and periodic statements that include the name or the logo of the bank or an affiliate.

Advertisements and brochures also should feature these disclosures at least as large as the text describing the bank's nondeposit investment products. The OCC believes that these disclosures are conspicuous when they appear on the cover of a brochure or on the first part of relevant written text. A bank's disclosures could also be considered conspicuous if it prints the required disclosures in a box or by displaying them in bold type or with bullet points.

The bank should obtain a signed statement acknowledging such disclosures from customers at the time a retail nondeposit investment account is opened. For accounts established before issuance of this section, the bank should consider obtaining such a signed statement prior to the next sale. If the bank solicits customers by telephone or mail, it should be assured that customers agreeing to purchase nondeposit investment products receive the disclosure acknowledgement form when they open a new account. A bank should also request all customers who previously opened investment accounts by mail without receiving these written disclosures to sign and return a disclosure acknowledgement to the bank.

Confirmations and account statements for nondeposit investment products should contain at least the minimum disclosures if the confirmation or account statement contains the name or logo of the bank or its affiliate. If a customer's periodic deposit account statement includes account information about nondeposit investment products, the bank should clearly separate that information from information about the deposit account. The material on the customer's periodic deposit account relating to nondeposit investment products also should begin with the disclosures described above as well as the identity of the entity conducting the nondeposit transaction.

Where applicable, examiners should determine that the bank has made additional disclosures described in the Interagency Statement regarding affiliate relationships and specific fees and penalties.

Some disclosure obligations may arise from the roles a bank or a bank affiliate may play in the distribution, administration, and/or management processes. For example, a bank should disclose remuneration received for performing investment advisory services and administrative services such as shareholder accounting. This disclosure obligation may be met through fee disclosures in a prospectus. If the prospectus does not include such fee disclosures, the bank must make the disclosures by some other means. State law requirements may also govern fee disclosures.

Additional disclosure responsibilities may occur because of the manner in which nondeposit investment products are marketed. Examiners should determine whether public statements about the selection of the products a bank offers are reasonable. As an example, if management represents to customers that it has performed an independent analysis of the product selected, the examiner should determine that the bank has actually done so. Examiners will also evaluate management's disclosure to prospective customers of ratings applicable to a particular product, including the source of the rating. If ratings are used to promote certain products, examiners should expect bank management to review whether the bank will disclose ratings changes and, if so, determine how such disclosures will occur.

Examiners should also determine whether a bank-related sales program includes any written or oral representations to customers concerning insurance coverage provided by any other entity apart from FDIC, e.g., the Securities Investor Protection Corporation (SIPC), a state insurance fund, or an insurance company. If these types of representations are made, examiners should determine whether training concerning differences in insurance coverage is provided to appropriate personnel. Appropriate personnel includes anyone who is likely to respond to customer inquiries or individuals designated to sell such products. Examiners should also determine if written or oral explanations of the differences in coverage are provided to all customers.

Advertising

Examiners should assess the procedures the bank uses to ensure that bank-related sales advertisements are accurate, do not mislead customers about the nature of the product, and include required disclosures. For example, claims about "no fees" or "no charges" are not accurate if the selling bank collects fees for investment advisory services or collects fees for shareholder accounting on the product or service being advertised. In this case a bank could claim that there are no "sales" charges and inform readers that a description of other charges is contained in the prospectus.

Examiners should determine that the bank does not imply in advertising or in written and oral presentations that the bank stands behind an investment product.

The bank's marketing department should not be solely responsible for bank-related investment sales advertisements. The issuer, or, if a mutual fund, the distributor, may prepare advertisements of specific investment products that conform to standards developed by self-regulatory organizations such as NASD. Senior bank management should appoint an officer responsible for ensuring that bank investment advertisements as well as advertisements prepared by another party that make reference to the bank, or any advertisement used in bank-related sales, are accurate, not misleading, and include all required disclosures.

Suitability

Consistent with the Rules of Fair Practice, the OCC expects banks to determine whether a product being recommended is an appropriate investment for the customer. Banks should ensure that any salespeople involved in bank-related sales obtain sufficient information from customers to enable the salesperson to make a judgment about the suitability of recommendations for particular customers. At a minimum, suitability inquiries should be made consistent with the Rules of Fair Practice concerning the customer's financial and tax status, investment objectives, and other factors that may be relevant, prior to making recommendations to the customer. This information should be documented and updated periodically.

A well-documented suitability inquiry can protect a bank from dissatisfied customers who threaten litigation. Such litigation could introduce risk to the bank's capital. Accordingly, the OCC may view banks operating a retail securities business without appropriate suitability procedures to be engaging in an unsafe and unsound practice.

Many banks use software programs that document investor profiles to assist in making suitability judgments. Each profile is based on a customer's responses to inquiries as to his or her financial and relevant personal history. The software program subsequently matches the customer's investment needs and objectives to the bank's available products. This type of software is a tool, not a substitute for professional judgement; it should not weight bank proprietary products too heavily or bank deposits too lightly.

One example of a critical suitability determination involves sales to elderly bank customers. Many of these customers rely upon investments or savings for retirement income and may consequently demand high yields. They may not, however, have the ability to absorb or recover losses. A nondeposit investment salesperson should also be aware that it is especially important to make a careful suitability recommendation when dealing with a surviving spouse who is not experienced in investment matters.

Examiners should investigate potential suitability problems in mutual fund sales when reviewing "breakpoints" and "letters of intent." Breakpoints are discounts that are available to investors who purchase a large amount of mutual fund shares in a lump sum or as part of a cumulative investment program (e.g., under a "letter of intent"). The potential for abuse usually occurs when the sale of several different mutual fund shares takes place in quantities just below the level at which the purchaser would qualify for reduced sales charges on any one of the funds.

Examiners should determine whether a bank officer has been assigned responsibility for implementing and/or monitoring the suitability system. The examination approach should focus on the system the bank has in place to make suitability inquiries, suitability judgements, and periodic account reviews. Examiners generally should review sales patterns rather than individual sales for suitability issues. To determine the types of sales to test for suitability, examiners should investigate marketing programs that target a class of customers, customer complaints, sales to first-time and risk-averse investors, sales made by high- or low-volume salespersons, volatile and new products, and the existence of mutual fund redemptions after relatively short holding periods.

Qualifications and Training

Banks should implement detailed training programs to ensure that sales personnel have thorough product knowledge (as opposed to simple sales training for a product) and understand customer protection requirements. Examiners should assess the process the bank uses to ensure that sales personnel are properly qualified and adequately trained to sell all bank-related nondeposit investment products. If bank personnel sell or recommend securities, the training should be substantively equivalent to that required for personnel qualified to sell securities as registered representatives. Securities industry training is available in most metropolitan areas.

Examiners also should determine that the bank's audit and compliance personnel and persons with supervisory responsibilities are properly trained and knowledgeable.

A bank's hiring practices and training plan should be designed around the complexity and risks of the particular investment products being offered. While it may be appropriate to have a banking generalist with no securities industry background sell money market mutual funds, it could be inappropriate to allow this individual to sell fixed-rate annuities without extensive training.

If individuals with securities industry experience are hired to sell investment products for banks, they should have an understanding of securities industry customer protection and control systems and have an adequate knowledge of the products being offered. Since they may not be familiar with general banking regulations and may not understand the needs of bank customers, banks should also ensure that these individuals are instructed as to the specialized obligations of selling investment products in a retail banking environment. Examiners should expect management to check with securities regulators to determine if potential bank sales employees with previous securities industry experience have a disciplinary history.

Banks engaging in lower volume mutual fund and annuity sales frequently train existing bank employees to sell investment products. Examiners should determine that bank management is satisfied that these individuals have acquired "product knowledge," and thoroughly understand the need to safeguard the customers' interests. More specialized "product knowledge" training is generally provided by the marketing division of a mutual fund sponsor or another third party vendor. Bank staff should also receive customer protection and compliance training.

Examiners should determine whether a bank officer has been assigned responsibility for ensuring that adequate training is provided to bank staff, and for reviewing the hiring and training practices of a third party vendor.

Compensation

Incentive compensation systems, which are standard in the securities and insurance businesses, are becoming increasingly common in commercial banking. Personnel who are authorized to sell nondeposit investment products may receive incentive compensation, such as commissions, for transactions entered into by customers. However, incentive compensation programs must not be structured in such a way as to result in unsuitable recommendations or sales being made to customers.

An improperly designed compensation system can provide a bank employee with the incentive to place his or her own compensation interests above the interests of bank customers. Examiners should assess the steps management has taken to ensure that compensation programs do not operate as an incentive for salespeople to make unsuitable recommendations or sales to customers.

One way to avoid having the compensation system drive the recommendation toward mutual funds and away from certificate of deposit renewals would be to separate the nondeposit investment product sales and CD renewal functions. Alternatively, if employees are permitted to offer both deposits and nondeposit investment products, a bank could reduce the temptation by compensating the employee for renewing maturing deposits as well as for selling nondeposit investment products. Examiners should discuss with bank management where appropriate the methods used to avoid possible conflicts of interest potentially arising from the bank's compensation plan.

To investigate whether incentive compensation schemes could induce salespersons to recommend products with higher commissions over a more suitable option, examiners should look to customer complaints and to sales patterns rather than to individual sales. For example, an examiner can look for instances in which sales for a particular product increased after changes to an incentive compensation system.

Examiners also should expect a bank to increase its supervision of sales programs as it increases its incentive compensation. Examiners should be critical of supervision that does not take into account the possibility that recommendations for purchases of nondeposit investment products could be influenced by the incentive compensation scheme.

If the overall setting and circumstances of a bank's investment sales program appears to be only marginally satisfactory, examiners should regard higher incentive compensation on certain investment products and lower compensation on deposits and other investment products as having the potential for causing serious problems. In this case the compensation system itself should justify an increase in the level of bank management supervision. If supervision is not adequate, the examiner should criticize the compensation system and other objectionable factors in the setting and circumstance of the sale.

Bank supervisory employees who review and approve individual sales, accept new accounts, and review established customer accounts should not receive incentive compensation based on the profitability of individual trades or accounts that are subject to their review. Similarly, department auditors or compliance personnel should not participate in incentive compensation programs that are based directly on the success of sales efforts nor should they report to a manager who receives this type of incentive compensation. In addition, bank management should not rely on third party audit and control systems if that vendor's control personnel receive transaction-based incentive compensation.

Bank employees, including tellers, may receive a one-time nominal fee of a fixed dollar amount for each customer referred for nondeposit investment products. The payment of this referral fee should not depend on whether the referral results in a transaction.

Fiduciary Accounts

Pursuant to 12 CFR 9.11(d), examiners will review the investments held by national banks as fiduciary to determine whether such investments are in accordance with law, 12 CFR 9, and sound fiduciary principles. In so doing, they will ensure that the bank has complied with all applicable state and federal restrictions on investment transactions involving the bank's fiduciary accounts.

Under 12 CFR 9.12, national bank fiduciaries may not invest funds held as fiduciary in the stock of organizations with which there exists such a connection as may affect the exercise of the best judgment of the bank in acquiring the stock, unless there exists specific authority for such an investment in the governing instrument, local law, a court order or through consents from all beneficiaries. As to accounts subject to the Employee Retirement Income Security Act of 1974, such investments must be within the authority of that Act. These principles govern purchases of a bank's proprietary products, such as bank-advised mutual funds and private label mutual funds for fiduciary accounts.

In addition, pursuant to 12 CFR 9.11(d), examiners will determine that fiduciary purchases and retention of bank proprietary products for fiduciary accounts are in accord with sound fiduciary principles. This requires that even if specific authority exists for fiduciary accounts to purchase or retain bank-advised or bank private label mutual funds, the assets must be appropriate for each account. The investment must be consistent with the purpose for which each account was created, and suitable for the beneficial interest holders of each account. This requirement exists as to purchases for individual accounts, and for conversions of collective investment funds to bank-advised mutual funds.

Twelve CFR 9.7 requires banks to conduct initial and annual reviews of each fiduciary account as well as a separate review of all securities by issuer to ensure compliance with these requirements. These reviews include:

• A documented review of each account to determine that the assets of that account, including any proprietary products, meet the investment objectives of the account. In structuring the account portfolio, the fiduciary must consider the provisions of the document establishing the account. The review must also take into account the needs of the beneficial interest holders. This review should address the issues set forth in the Comptroller's Handbook for Fiduciary Activities, "Portfolio Management."

- A documented annual review of all assets by issuer, including proprietary products. This review should consider the quality of fund management, fee structure, risk diversification and anticipated rates of return. It should also address the considerations set forth in the Comptroller's Handbook for Fiduciary Activities, "Investments."

Compliance Program

Banks must maintain compliance programs capable of verifying compliance with the guidelines specified in the Interagency Statement and with any other applicable requirements. Banks should perform nondeposit investment compliance programs independently of investment product sales and management. At a minimum, the compliance function should include a system to monitor customer complaints and to review customer accounts periodically to detect and prevent abusive practices.

Examiners reviewing the compliance operations of a bank offering a variety of retail investment products should ensure that the bank has comprehensive self-regulatory policies and that it is conducting an ongoing comparison of the bank's investment sales practices with its stated investment policy. In banks with a less elaborate investment sales program, where an internal auditing group may perform all of the bank's compliance functions, the examiner should ensure that these auditors are periodically comparing sales practices with policy.

Individuals performing the audit or compliance of the bank's investment program should be qualified and should have the necessary experience to perform the assigned tasks. Compliance personnel should also engage in ongoing training to keep abreast of emerging developments in banking and securities laws and regulations.

Banks can establish independence of audit or compliance personnel if such personnel determine the scope, frequency, and depth of their own reviews; report their findings directly to the board of directors or an appropriate committee of the board; have their performance evaluated by persons independent of the investment product sales function; and receive compensation that is not connected to the success of investment product sales.

Bank compliance programs should be modeled after those in the securities business where it is customary for compliance personnel to conduct regular and frequent customer account reviews in order to detect and prevent abuses. The extent and frequency of customer account supervision should be dictated by the aggressiveness of the sales program and the riskiness of products being offered.

Examiners should expect the bank to assign individuals independent of the sales force to review periodically customer responses to suitability inquiries and to compare these responses to the type and volume of account activity to determine whether the activity in an account is appropriate. If account activity is unusual relative to the customer's stated objectives and risk tolerance, or if account activity is brisk relative to the size of a customer's investment or past practices, management should make follow-up inquiries to determine if the activity serves the best interests of the customer.

If examinations or routine oversight by bank management indicates that suitability problems may exist, bank management is expected to conduct its own review of all affected accounts and to institute corrective actions. If it is determined that customers may have been disadvantaged, corrective actions should be designed on a case-by-case basis and may include full explanations to customers and, where appropriate, offers to rescind trades.

Customer complaints are an indication of potential problems that warrant a prompt account review. Examiners should expect the bank to assign a bank officer who is independent of the sales force the responsibility for approving the resolution of complaints or reviewing the resolution of complaints by a third party vendor. The examiner should evaluate the system for assuring that all complaints (written and oral) receive management's attention by reviewing the bank's audit of the complaint resolution system.

Managers of high-volume investment sales programs also often use automated exception reporting systems to flag potential problems before customers complain. Such systems monitor product sales and the performance of salespersons. If the bank has such systems in place, and if the reports show significant volumes of mutual fund redemptions after short holding periods, examiners should review the steps management has taken to investigate whether the product is being sold properly.

If early redemptions are restricted to one salesperson or one branch, management can reasonably conclude that the problem is localized. However, early redemptions occurring throughout the sales network may indicate that something is wrong with the product itself or with the training provided to salespeople. Similarly, if reports indicate that a salesperson is selling one type of product almost exclusively, management may need to review that individual's performance or training.

Ultimately, the way for bank management to assure itself that the securities salespersons are providing the required disclosures and making suitable recommendations to customers is to "test" the sales program. Effective "tests" can be conducted in several ways. Larger banks sometimes employ "testers" who pose as prospective customers and test the sales presentations for a variety of issues including adherence to customer protection standards. Many other well-managed banks (of all sizes) have instituted follow-up programs to verify that their customers understood their investment transactions. A bank manager, who is independent of the sales force, may telephone customers a few days after an investment account is opened or an unusual transaction has taken place. The manager will determine if the customer understands what he or she has purchased; understands the risks, including the uninsured nature of the product; understands the bank's role in the transaction; and can generally confirm responses to a suitability inquiry previously provided.

A bank officer usually can determine if a customer understands an investment by asking the customer to describe its general features. The customer should be able to describe how the product works and its risks rather than simply recite what he or she hopes to gain from the particular investment. Managers usually also determine if the customer is satisfied with the product and service or has any problems or suggestions for improving service. If a bank institutes a telephone follow-up program, it should maintain a record of conversations with customers to resolve problems or disputes that may arise at a later date.

"Negative consent" letters (i.e., notices informing customers that unless they object, the bank assumes the customer understands and does not object to the transactions) may be a useful element in a compliance program, but should not be the sole means of verifying that customers understand nondeposit investment product transactions and the bank's role in the process.

Examiners should determine whether a bank officer has been assigned the responsibility for assuring that the bank adequately monitors the nondeposit investment accounts of customers. Examiners should also determine whether the officer has developed or is developing a system to monitor the customer account reviews of outside vendors operating bank-related sales programs.

Oversight of Third Party Vendors

When a bank uses a third party vendor to sell nondeposit investment products, the bank's board of directors must adopt a written policy addressing the scope of the activities of the third party, as well as the procedures the bank intends to use for monitoring the third party's compliance with the Interagency Statement.

To select the third party vendor and monitor the ongoing acceptability of the vendor, bank management usually reviews the vendor's experience in the business and the vendor's financial statement. Bank management also usually contacts other banks with which the vendor has done business for references. Examiners should also expect that bank management checked with the vendor's regulator before it entered into an agreement with the vendor and that management has continued to review reports furnished to the vendor by its regulators).

Bank management should enter into a written agreement with a third party vendor that has been approved by the bank's board of directors before the vendor is permitted to offer nondeposit investment products to the bank's customers. The agreement should outline the duties and responsibilities of each party and should include a description of all of the activities the third party is permitted to engage in on the bank's premises. The agreement also should set forth terms for the use of the bank's space, personnel, and equipment as well as compensation arrangements for personnel of the bank and the third party. The agreement also should:

- Specify that the third party will comply with all applicable laws and regulations and will act consistently with the provisions of this temporary insert, especially the provisions relating to customer disclosures,
- Authorize the bank to monitor the third party by periodically reviewing and verifying that the third party and its sales representatives are complying with its agreement with the bank, with all applicable laws and regulations, and with the provisions of this temporary insert,
- Specify the type, scope, and frequency of reports the third party is to furnish

to bank management to permit bank management to fulfill its oversight responsibilities,

- Authorize the institution and the OCC to have access to appropriate records of the third party,
- Require the third party to agree to indemnify the bank for any liability that resulted from third party investment product sales program actions,
- Set forth the training which the bank expects its employees and third party personnel to possess, and
- Provide for written employment contracts between the bank and the third party vendor's employees.

Examiners will review the agreement to determine that it specifies that the third party vendor will comply with all applicable requirements contained in the Interagency Statement. Examiners also will review the agreement to determine if it includes provisions regarding bank oversight and examiner access to appropriate records. It is expected that compliance with the agreement will be periodically monitored by the institution's senior management.

Before entering into an agreement with a third party vendor, bank management also should be satisfied that the vendor uses a product selection process similar to the one outlined below. Banks relying on a third party vendor to select products also should understand and agree with the vendor's method of analysis and document its concurrence with that method. Examiners should determine whether management has understood and concurred. Bank management should periodically investigate the vendor's product selection process to ensure that it continues to be appropriate to the bank's customer mix. Examiners also should determine whether bank management understands and agrees with contingency plans developed by the third party vendor and the product issuer to respond to customer orders during unusual surges in redemptions.

To fulfill its oversight responsibilities, it is expected that bank management will receive various reports from the third party vendor and have access to the vendor's appropriate records. The reports received will vary with the scope of the sales program and should be tailored to the needs of the institution. The reports should always include a list of all customer complaints and their resolution. Other reports that may facilitate bank management's oversight role, could include:

- A periodic listing of all new account openings and descriptions of the initial trades;
- A list of significant or unusual (for the customer) individual sales during a reporting period;
- Sales reports by product, salesperson, and location during a reporting period; and
- Reports of internal compliance reviews of customer accounts originated at the bank and reports furnished to the third party vendor by its regulator(s) on at least an annual basis.

Bank management must monitor compliance by third party vendors on an ongoing basis. Senior bank managers will be expected to ensure that specific individuals employed by the bank and by the third party vendor are responsible for each activity outlined in the bank's investment sales policy. The degree of bank management's involvement should be dictated by the types of products being offered, the volume of sales, the nature of customers' complaints, and the effectiveness of the third party vendor's customer protection systems.

Senior bank management also should appoint an officer responsible for ensuring that bank investment advertisements as well as advertisements prepared by another party that refer to the bank, or any advertisement used in bank-related sales, are accurate, not misleading, and include all required disclosures. In addition, any advertising or promotional material — prepared by or on behalf of a third party vendor — should clearly identify the company selling the nondeposit investment product and should not suggest that the depository institution is the seller.

Examiner access to the records of third party vendors should be governed by preliminary examination findings. When such findings make it clear that bank management has discharged its oversight responsibility by reviewing and responding appropriately to third party reports, only a few customer complaints have been filed against the vendor, and the vendor's reports are timely, sufficiently detailed, and prepared by someone independent of the vendor's sales force, examiner access to third party records should generally be limited to the reports furnished to management by the vendor.

Product Selection

This section describes in general terms the methods that well-managed banks use to select specific nondeposit investment products and to determine that such products continue to be acceptable to the bank's customer mix. This information is provided to help examiners understand and review the process used by well-managed banks to make this determination.

Bank management should determine the specific laws, regulations, regulatory conditions or other limitations or requirements, including qualitative considerations, that will govern the sale of products to be offered. Although not required, most well-run bank investment sales programs limit the number of products offered so that customers and salespersons will not be presented with an overwhelming number of choices. Limitations based on product quality may also make it easier for sales managers to shield certain classes of customers from inappropriate products.

As a general practice, bank investment programs offer at least one type of money market mutual fund for customers who are interested in liquidity. In addition, most banks offer a U.S. government bond fund for customers who stress safety and steady income, an equity fund for customers interested in capital growth, and a tax-exempt bond fund for customers who wish to avoid taxes on investment earnings.

When deciding which funds to offer, managers should review the fund's performance over an extended period of time. Most bank managers prefer to avoid mutual funds with volatile records. Management's selection of a family of funds should not be based on the performance of one particular fund; each fund selection should stand on its own merits.

Management's selection of investment products usually begins with an evaluation of the stability of asset values over time and an assessment of yields to investors. Management also compares the performance of other funds with similar objectives over the same period(s). Specialized ratings services (such as Morningstar or Lipper) or rankings by analytical services are usually regarded as necessary but secondary considerations.

Management also considers the fund's track record in terms of both risk and reward. Management analyzes the fund's net asset value versus total return, its management or operating expenses, the turnover within the fund's portfolio, and capital gains and other sources of income. Other key considerations include the composition of the portfolio and concentrations in types of holdings, sector weights, and, in the case of equity funds, the percentage of ownership represented by individual issues.

Management also evaluates important non-statistical factors such as the continuity, tenure, and demonstrated talent of the fund's management. They also may consider factors such as the quality of a mutual fund's operational and marketing support.

The bank itself, and not another entity's marketing department, should select the funds to be offered. Independent committees and qualified analysts should make the final selections, not a sales manager whose view of the commission structure may affect this judgment.

If the bank uses outside consultants to help select a mutual fund, bank management should determine whether the consultant receives compensation from mutual funds or mutual fund wholesalers. If the analysis is performed by another party, such as a clearing broker or third party vendor, bank management should understand and agree with the method of analysis and should document the bank's concurrence.

Regardless of who selects the mutual fund products, bank management will be expected to consider the issuer's contingency plans for handling unusual surges in redemptions at the time such products are being considered. Such contingency plans normally include emergency staffing, communications, and operational programs that are based on various market scenarios.

Bank management should compare these contingency plans to the expected needs of bank customers during periods of stress.

Finally, once the initial selection process is complete, bank management should conduct ongoing reviews to assure that the products remain acceptable in light of the bank's objectives and customer's needs.

Selection of annuity products is conducted in the same manner. A variable-rate annuity, a hybrid form of investment that contains elements of mutual funds and insurance, could be characterized as a mutual fund operated by an insurance company. During product selection, bank management should consider the performance and composition of the portfolio that is dedicated to the annuity holders.

Selection analysis for fixed-rate annuities differs from variable-rate annuities. Since fixed-rate annuities are obligations of insurance companies, the risks associated with them relate to the issuer's ability to honor the terms of the annuity contract. Accordingly, the safety of an annuity depends upon the financial standing of the firm that issues it and the selection analysis involves an assessment of the quality and diversification of the company's assets, its holdings of junk bonds, mortgage-backed securities, and problem real estate loans, as well as the continuity of management.

Because it is difficult to independently analyze insurance companies, ratings provided by rating agencies such as A.M. Best, Standard & Poor's, Duff & Phelps, Moody's and Weiss Research play a part in annuity analysis. If bank management relies significantly on such ratings rather than on its own analysis, however, examiners should expect that the issuer selected by the bank has received top ratings from most of the ratings services.

When analyzing annuities, management also should recognize that an issuing insurance company can, in certain circumstances, sell or simply transfer the annuity contract to another insurance company, thereby extinguishing its obligation to the purchaser of the annuity. Annuity owners are generally, but not always, asked to consent to this transfer. A bank selling annuities should consider the possibility of such a transfer in its product selection analysis. At a minimum, the bank should disclose this possibility to prospective customers.

Interagency Statement on Retail Sales of Nondeposit Investment Products

February 15, 1994

Introduction

Recently many insured depository institutions have expanded their activities in recommending or selling to retail customers nondeposit investment products, such as mutual funds and annuities. Many depository institutions are providing these services at the retail level, directly or through various types of arrangements with third parties.

Sales activities for nondeposit investment products should ensure that customers for these products are clearly and fully informed of the nature and risks associated with these products. In particular, where nondeposit investment products are recommended or sold to retail customers, depository institutions should ensure that customers are fully informed that the products:

- Are not insured by the FDIC;
- Are not deposits or other obligations of the institution and are not guaranteed by the institution; and,
- Are subject to investment risks, including possible loss of principal invested.

Moreover, sales activities involving these investment products should be designed to minimize the possibility of customer confusion and to safeguard the institution from liability under the applicable anti-fraud provisions of the federal securities laws, which, among other things, prohibit materially misleading or inaccurate representations in connection with the sale of securities.

The four federal banking agencies — the Board of Governors of the Federal Reserve System, the Federal Deposit Insurance Corporation, the Office of the Comptroller of the Currency, and the Office of Thrift Supervision — are issuing this Statement to provide uniform guidance to depository institutions engaging in these activities.

(Note: Each of the four banking agencies has in the past issued guidelines addressing various aspects of the retail sale of nondeposit investment products. OCC Banking Circular 274 (July 1 9, 1993); FDIC Supervisory Statement FIL-71-93 (October 8, 1993); Federal Reserve Letters SR 93-35 (June 17, 1993), and SR 91-14 (June 6, 1991); OTS Thrift Bulletin 23-1 (September 7, 1993). This Statement is intended to consolidate and make uniform the guidance contained in the various existing statements of each of the agencies, all of which are superseded by this Statement. Some of the banking agencies have adopted additional guidelines covering the sale of certain specific types of instruments by depository institutions, i.e., obligations of the institution itself or of an affiliate of the institution. These guidelines remain in effect except where clearly inapplicable.)

Scope

This Statement applies when retail recommendations or sales of nondeposit investment products are made by:

- Employees of the depository institution;
- Employees of a third party, which may or may not be affiliated with the institution (see Note, below, addressing which institutions are covered), occurring on the premises of the institution (including telephone sales or recommendations by employees or from the institution's premises and sales or recommendations initiated by mail from its premises); and
- Sales resulting from a referral of retail customers by the institution to a third party when the depository institution receives a benefit for the referral.

(Note: This Statement does not apply to the subsidiaries of insured state nonmember banks, which are subject to separate provisions, contained in 12 CFR 337.4, relating to securities activities. For OTS-regulated institutions that conduct sales of nondeposit investment products through a subsidiary, these guidelines apply to the subsidiary. 12 CFR 545.74 also applies to such sales. Branches and agencies of U.S. foreign banks should follow these guidelines with respect to their nondeposit investment sales programs.)

These guidelines generally do not apply to the sale of nondeposit investment products to non-retail customers, such as sales to fiduciary accounts administered by an institution. (Note: Restrictions on a national bank's use as fiduciary of the bank's brokerage service or other entity with which the bank has a conflict of interest, including purchases of the bank's proprietary and other products, are set out in 12 CFR 9.12. Similar restrictions on transactions between funds held by a federal savings association as fiduciary and any person or organization with whom there exists an interest that might affect the best judgment of the association acting in its fiduciary capacity are set out in 12 CFR 550.10. However, as part of its fiduciary responsibility, an institution should take appropriate steps to avoid potential customer confusion when providing nondeposit investment products to the institution's fiduciary customers.)

Adoption of Policies and Procedures

Program Management. A depository institution involved in the activities described above for the sale of nondeposit investment products to its retail customers should adopt a written statement that addresses the risks associated with the sales program and contains a summary of policies and procedures outlining the features of the institution's program and addressing, at a minimum, the concerns described in this Statement. The written statement should address the scope of activities of any third party involved, as well as the procedures for monitoring compliance by third parties in accordance with the guidelines below. The scope and level of detail of the statement should appropriately reflect the level of the institution's involvement in the sale or recommendation of nondeposit investment products. The institution's statement should be adopted and reviewed periodically by its board of directors. Depository institutions are encouraged to consult with legal counsel with regard to the implementation of a nondeposit investment product sales program.

The institution's policies and procedures should include the following:

- Compliance procedures. The procedures for ensuring compliance with applicable laws and regulations and consistency with the provisions of this Statement.
- Supervision of personnel involved in sales. A designation by senior managers of specific individuals to exercise supervisory responsibility for each activity outlined in the institution's policies and procedures.
- Types of products sold. The criteria governing the selection and review of each type of product sold or recommended.
- Permissible use of customer information. The procedures for the use of

information regarding the institution's customers for any purpose in connection with the retail sale of nondeposit investment products.

- Designation of employees to sell investment products. A description of the responsibilities of those personnel authorized to sell nondeposit investment products and of other personnel who may have contact with retail customers concerning the sales program, and a description of any appropriate and inappropriate referral activities and the training requirements and compensation arrangements for each class of personnel.

Arrangements with Third Parties. If a depository institution directly or indirectly, including through a subsidiary or service corporation, engages in activities as described above under which a third party sells or recommends nondeposit investment products, the institution should, prior to entering into the arrangement, conduct an appropriate review of the third party. The institution should have a written agreement with the third party that is approved by the institution's board of directors. Compliance with the agreement should be periodically monitored by the institution's senior management. At a minimum, the written agreement should:

- Describe the duties and responsibilities of each party, including a description of permissible activities by the third party on the institution's premises, terms as to the use of the institution's space, personnel, and equipment, and compensation arrangements for personnel of the institution and the third party.
- Specify that the third party will comply with all applicable laws and regulations, and will act consistently with the provisions of this Statement and, in particular, with the provisions relating to customer disclosures.
- Authorize the institution to monitor the third party and periodically review and verify that the third party and its sales representatives are complying with its agreement with the institution.
- Authorize the institution and the appropriate banking agency to have access to such records of the third party as are necessary or appropriate to evaluate such compliance.
- Require the third party to indemnify the institution for potential liability resulting from actions of the third party with regard to the investment product sales program.
- Provide for written employment contracts, satisfactory to the institution, for personnel who are employees of both the institution and the third party.

General Guidelines

1. Disclosures and Advertising

The banking agencies believe that recommending or selling nondeposit investment products to retail customers should occur in a manner that assures that the products are clearly differentiated from insured deposits. Conspicuous and easy to comprehend disclosures concerning the nature of nondeposit investment products and the risk inherent in investing in these products are one of the most important ways of ensuring that the differences between nondeposit products and insured deposits are understood.

Content and Form of Disclosure. Disclosures with respect to the sale or recommendation of these products should, at a minimum, specify that the product is:

- Not insured by the FDIC;
- Not a deposit or other obligation of, or guaranteed by, the depository institution;
- Subject to investment risks, including possible loss of the principal amount invested.

The written disclosures described above should be conspicuous and presented in a clear and concise manner. Depository institutions may provide any additional disclosures that further clarify the risks involved with particular nondeposit investment products.

Timing of Disclosure. The minimum disclosures should be provided to the customer:

- Orally during any sales presentation,
- Orally when investment advice concerning nondeposit investment products is provided,
- Orally and in writing prior to or at the time an investment account is opened to purchase these products, and
- In advertisements and other promotional materials, as described below.

A statement, signed by the customer should be obtained at the time such an account is opened, acknowledging that the customer has received and understands the disclosures. For investment accounts established prior to the issuance of these guidelines, the institution should consider obtaining such a signed statement at the time of the next transaction.

Confirmations and account statements for such products should contain at least the minimum disclosures if the confirmations or account statements contain the name or the logo of the depository institution or an affiliate. (Note: These disclosures should be made in addition to any other confirmation disclosures that are required by law or regulation, e.g., 12 CFR 12, 208.8(k)(3), and 344.) If a customer's periodic deposit account statement includes account information concerning the customer's nondeposit investment products, the information concerning these products should be clearly separate from the information concerning the deposit account, and should be introduced with the minimum disclosures and the identity of the entity conducting the nondeposit transaction.

Advertisements and Other Promotional Material. Advertisements and other promotional and sales material, written or otherwise, about nondeposit investment products sold to retail customers should conspicuously include at least the minimum disclosures discussed above and must not suggest or convey any inaccurate or misleading impression about the nature of the product or its lack of FDIC insurance. The minimum disclosures should also be emphasized in telemarketing contacts. Any third party advertising or promotional material should clearly identify the company selling the nondeposit investment product and should not suggest that the depository institution is the seller. If brochures, signs, or other written material contain information about both FDIC-insured deposits and nondeposit investment products, these materials should clearly segregate information about nondeposit investment products from the information about deposits.

Additional Disclosures. Where applicable, the depository institution should disclose the existence of an advisory or other material relationship between the institution or an affiliate of the institution and an investment company whose shares are sold by the institution and any material relationship between the institution and an affiliate involved in providing nondeposit investment products. In addition, where applicable, the existence of any fees, penalties, or surrender charges should be disclosed. These additional disclosures should be made prior to or at the time an investment account is opened to purchase these products.

If sales activities include any written or oral representations concerning insurance coverage provided by any entity other than the FDIC, e.g., the Securities Investor Protection Corporation (SIPC), a state insurance fund, or a private insurance company, then clear and accurate written or oral explanations of the coverage must also be provided to customers when the representations concerning insurance coverage are made, in order to minimize possible confusion with FDIC insurance. Such representations should not suggest or imply that any alternative insurance coverage is the same as or similar to FDIC insurance.

Because of the possibility of customer confusion, a nondeposit investment product must not have a name that is identical to the name of the depository institution. Recommending or selling a nondeposit investment product with a name similar to that of the depository institution should only occur pursuant to a sales program designed to minimize the risk of customer confusion. The institution should take appropriate steps to assure that the issuer of the product has complied with any applicable requirements established by the Securities and Exchange Commission regarding the use of similar names.

2. Setting and Circumstances

Selling or recommending nondeposit investment products on the premises of a depository institution may give the impression that the products are FDIC-insured or are obligations of the depository institution. To minimize customer confusion with deposit products, sales or recommendations of nondeposit investment products on the premises of a depository institution should be conducted in a physical location distinct from the area where retail deposits are taken. Signs or other means should be used to distinguish the investment sales area from the retail deposit-taking area of the institution. However, in the limited situation where physical considerations prevent sales of nondeposit products from being conducted in a distinct area, the institution has a heightened responsibility to ensure appropriate measures are in place to minimize customer confusion.

In no case, however, should tellers and other employees, while located in the routine deposit-taking area, such as the teller window, make general or specific investment recommendations regarding nondeposit investment products, qualify a customer as eligible to purchase such products, or accept orders for such products, even if unsolicited. Tellers and other employees who are not authorized to sell nondeposit investment products may refer customers to individuals who are specifically designated and trained to assist customers interested in the purchase of such products.

3. Qualifications and Training

The depository institution should ensure that its personnel who are authorized to sell nondeposit investment products or to provide investment advice with respect to such products are adequately trained with regard to the specific products being sold or recommended. Training should not be limited to sales methods, but should impart a thorough knowledge of the products involved, of applicable legal restrictions, and of customer protection requirements. If depository institution personnel sell or recommend securities, the training should be the substantive equivalent of that required for personnel qualified to sell securities as registered representatives. (Note: Savings associations are not exempt from the definitions of "broker" and "dealer" in Sections 3(a)(4) and 3(a)(5) of the Securities Exchange Act of 1934; therefore, all securities sales personnel in savings associations must be registered representatives.)

Depository institution personnel with supervisory responsibilities should receive training appropriate to that position. Training should also be provided to employees of the depository institution who have direct contact with customers to ensure a basic understanding of the institution's sales activities and the policy of limiting the involvement of employees who are not authorized to sell investment products to customer referrals. Training should be updated periodically and should occur on an ongoing basis.

Depository institutions should investigate the backgrounds of employees hired for their nondeposit investment products sales programs, including checking for possible disciplinary actions by securities and other regulators if the employees have previous investment industry experience.

4. Suitability and Sales Practices

Depository institution personnel involved in selling nondeposit investment products must adhere to fair and reasonable sales practices and be subject to effective management and compliance reviews with regard to such practices. In this regard, if depository institution personnel recommend nondeposit investment products to customers, they should have reasonable grounds for believing that the specific product recommended is suitable for the particular customer on the basis of information disclosed by the customer. Personnel should make reasonable efforts to obtain information directly from the customer regarding, at a minimum, the customer's financial and tax status, investment objectives, and other information that may be useful or reasonable in making investment recommendations to that customer. This information should be documented and updated periodically.

5. Compensation

Depository institution employees, including tellers, may receive a one-time nominal fee of a fixed dollar amount for each customer referral for nondeposit investment products. The payment of this referral fee should not depend on whether the referral results in a transaction.

Personnel who are authorized to sell nondeposit investment products may receive incentive compensation, such as commissions, for transactions entered into by customers. However, incentive compensation programs must not be structured in such a way as to result in unsuitable recommendations or sales being made to customers.

Depository institution compliance and audit personnel should not receive incentive compensation directly related to results of the nondeposit investment sales program.

6. Compliance

Depository institutions should develop and implement policies and procedures to ensure that nondeposit investment product sales activities are conducted in compliance with applicable laws and regulations, the institution's internal policies and procedures, and in a manner consistent with this Statement. Compliance procedures should identify any potential conflicts of interest and how such conflicts should be addressed. The compliance procedures should also provide for a system to monitor customer complaints and their resolution. Where applicable, compliance procedures also should call for verification that third party sales are being conducted in a manner consistent with the governing agreement with the depository institution.

The compliance function should be conducted independently of nondeposit investment product sales and management activities. Compliance personnel should determine the scope and frequency of their own review, and findings of compliance reviews should be periodically reported directly to the institution's board of directors, or to a designated committee of the board. Appropriate procedures for the nondeposit investment product programs should also be incorporated into the institution's audit program.

Supervision by Banking Agencies

The federal banking agencies will continue to review a depository institution's policies and procedures governing recommendations and sales of nondeposit investment products, as well as management's implementation and compliance with such policies and all other applicable requirements. The banking agencies will monitor compliance with the institution's policies and procedures by third parties that participate in the sale of these products. The failure of a depository institution to establish and observe appropriate policies and procedures consistent with this Statement in connection with sales activities involving nondeposit investment products will be subject to criticism and appropriate corrective action.

Questions on the Statement may be submitted to:

FRB — Division of Banking Supervision and Regulation, Securities Regulation Section, (202) 452-2781; Legal Division, (202) 452-2246.

FDIC — Office of Policy, Division of Supervision, (202) 898-6759; Regulation and Legislation Section, Legal Division (202) 898-3796.

OCC — Office of the Chief National Bank Examiner, Capital Markets Group, (202) 874-5070.

OTS — Office of Supervision Policy, (202) 906-5740; Corporate and Securities Division, (202) 906-7289.

Effective date: February 15, 1994

Retail Nondeposit Investment Sales (Section 413)

Examination Procedures

All examiners should be familiar with all examination procedures, and should complete any steps they think are necessary. However, there are some reasonable standards for which procedures form the basis of review of certain types of operations:

For a community bank that uses an independent third party vendor to operate its retail sales program, examiners may find it adequate to complete only the Third Party Vendor section of the ICQs and the related examination procedures.

For a bank that operates its own sales program or operates through a joint venture or an affiliated broker/dealer , an examiner will usually find it necessary to complete all sections at the first examination. At subsequent examinations of sales programs with no apparent weaknesses, completion of only the core examination procedures (indicated in bold type) may be adequate. Any concern that surfaces when applying the core procedures may be addressed by expanding the examination.

1. Complete the Internal Control Questionnaire (ICQ). Note explanations for any negative answers and changes since the last examination.

Scope of the Examination

2. To determine the scope of the examination:

    a. Meet with senior management of the bank or department to discuss the scope and direction of the retail nondeposit investment sales program.

    b. Review the business plan and policy and procedure manual to gain perspective on the nature of the bank's program. Note any significant changes since the last examination.

c. Review compliance and/or audit coverage and reports since the last examination. Note:

    – Previously identified strengths and weaknesses, and
    – Responses to criticisms in previous audit/compliance and examination reports.

Program Management

3.   Determine the extent of management involvement in the operation, and the quality of management of the retail nondeposit investment sales program. Review:

- Responses to the Program Management section of the ICQ.
- Resumes of key officials involved in the management of the sales program to determine their experience and tenure with the bank.
- Written performance objectives and performance appraisals of key management personnel to determine whether objectives and appraisals incorporate compliance issues, particularly compliance with disclosure and customer protection standards.
- Reports furnished to senior management and the board of directors to determine whether they are sufficiently timely, accurate and meaningful to permit effective oversight.

4.   Review senior management's actions in implementing the retail nondeposit investment sales program and in offering any new products. Specifically determine whether bank management:

- Participated in the development of the bank's investment sales program strategic plan.
- Conducted a risk and regulatory assessment and adopted a compliance program directed at ensuring compliance with all applicable laws, rules, regulations, regulatory conditions, and the Interagency Statement's guidelines.
- Provided for internal audit/compliance participation in the development of the program.
- Adopted a program management statement aimed at ensuring effective supervision of the individuals engaged in sales activities — whether they are employees of the bank or of another entity involved

in bank-related sales of investment products.

5. Determine how the retail nondeposit investment sales program is managed.

    a. Analyze sales program growth and earnings performance and determine why certain products have high levels of performance. Consider how this performance relates to incentive compensation and the suitability of recommendations to customers.

    b. Review the customer mix and market surveys. Look at trends in identifiable classes of customers and be alert for concentrations by types of customers. Also, try to determine whether customers are viewed as one-time buyers or are being cultivated to establish longer term relationships.

    c. Review the products offered and any market surveys and determine the risk inherent in different products. Consider whether management has attempted to match products to investors' needs in general.

    d. Review projections for the sales program and for different products and determine whether they:

        – Are realistic in light of the bank's customer mix;
        – Relate to bank staffing and training plans for the sales, supervision, and compliance functions; and
        – Are consistent with the bank's overall strategic plan.

    e. Determine the effectiveness of the bank's self-regulatory policies and procedures as measured by the number and type of customer complaints and by responses to the ICQ.

Product Selection

6. Assess the adequacy of management processes to select and review products sold. Review:

    • Responses to the Product Selection section of the ICQ.

- Methods bank management uses to select products to meet customer needs.
- Management's comparison of the performance of the products they offer to general market products with similar objectives.

7. Discuss your findings from the product selection review with senior management and make a judgement about the appropriateness of management's decision to continue to offer these products.

Use of Customer Information

8. Determine whether policies governing the permissible uses of bank customer information address the steps to be taken to reduce possible confusion among depositors who are being solicited to purchase nondeposit investment products.

Setting and Circumstances of Sales

9. Determine whether bank management has established effective controls to distinguish retail deposit-taking activities from retail nondeposit investment sales. Consider how the various elements of the setting and circumstances may interact to influence the customers' perception.

10. Where the deposit-taking and securities sale functions are performed by the same personnel, determine if the bank uses appropriate written and oral disclosures to guard against customer confusion, and the extent to which bank staff is trained to use, and does use, such disclosures.

Disclosures and Advertising

11. Review responses to the Disclosures and Advertising section of the ICQ and a representative sample of each type of advertising and promotional material.

  a. Determine whether all of the required disclosures are featured conspicuously in:

   - All written or oral sales presentations,

- Advertising and promotional materials,
- Confirmations and account statements that contain the name or the logo of the bank or an affiliate, and
- Periodic statements that include information on both deposit and nondeposit products.

b. Determine, where applicable, if the bank has disclosed the existence of:

- An advisory or other relationship between the bank and any affiliate involved in providing nondeposit investment products, and
- Any early withdrawal penalties, surrender charge penalties, and deferred sales charges.

c. Determine whether bank-related sales advertisements are:

- Accurate, and
- Not likely to mislead customers about the nature of the product.

d. Review product brochures and advertising to ensure that they do not imply that the bank stands behind an investment product. Also determine whether public statements concerning the selection of the products a bank offers are reasonable.

e. Determine whether personnel make any written or oral representations concerning insurance coverage by any entity other than the FDIC, e.g., Securities Investor Protection Corporation (SIPC); a state insurance fund; or an insurance company.

If representations about non-FDIC insurance coverage are made, determine whether:

- Each appropriate person who has contact with customers is trained concerning the differences among those coverages, and
- Written or oral explanations of the differences in coverage are provided to all customers.

Suitability

12. Judge whether systems in place are adequate to ensure that sales personnel make suitable recommendations and whether management is discharging its responsibilities under these systems by reviewing:

   - Responses to the Suitability section of the ICQ,
   - Customer complaints and resolutions,
   - Sales patterns,
   - Compensation differentials that may influence recommendations, and
   - Compliance and/or audit reports.

13. If your findings in 12, above, are negative or uncertain, review a sample of sales to determine if transactions appear unsuitable for a customer, based on responses to the suitability inquiries. The sample should include transactions involving:

   - Customer complaints,
   - Marketing programs that target a class of customers,
   - First-time and risk-averse investors,
   - High or low volume salespersons,
   - More volatile and newer products, and
   - Redemptions of annuities or mutual funds after relatively short holding periods.

14. If, after the review in 13, above, you are still not certain that recommendations are suitable, direct bank management to conduct an independent review of all affected accounts and to report their findings to the EIC.

15. If you determine that customers may have been disadvantaged, discuss appropriate corrective action with senior management. Such action should be designed on a case by case basis and may include:

   - Full explanations to customers and, where appropriate, offers to rescind trade.
   - A recommendation to bring in an independent audit or special

counsel to perform further review of customer transactions.
- Other action agreed upon between bank management and the EIC.

Qualifications and Training

16. Assess the bank's process for ensuring that supervisory, investment sales, audit, and compliance personnel are properly qualified and adequately trained by reviewing hiring and training practices and future plans and determining whether they are:

- Designed around the complexity and risks of the investment products being offered, and
- Consistent with the organization's projections for growth and product line expansion.

Compensation

17. Review the compensation plan and assess the steps management has taken to ensure that compensation programs are not structured in a way that result in unsuitable recommendations or sales being made to customers.

   a. Be alert to increases in the sales volume of a particular product, to customer complaints, and to suitability problems that may relate to the incentive compensation system and/or changes in compensation.

   b. Determine whether supervision of sales programs or of individual product offerings increases as incentive compensation increases.

   c. Determine whether referral fees are, in any way, based on a sale being made.

   d. Review written performance objectives and a sample of performance appraisals for salespersons and determine if the system for motivating and rewarding salespersons strikes a reasonable balance between profitability and the need to protect customer interests.

Sales to Fiduciary Accounts

18. Determine whether, on retail nondeposit investment transactions involving the bank's fiduciary accounts, the bank has complied with all applicable state and federal restrictions, including the Employee Retirement Income Security Act of 1974.

    a. If proprietary or private label sales to trust accounts were executed through the bank's nondeposit investment sales program, determine if the transactions were expressly authorized under state law or if authorization were obtained by the bank.

    b. Determine whether management's justification of any transfer of trust account investments to investments acquired through the bank's nondeposit investment sales program has taken into account all relevant circumstances, account by account. Relevant circumstances include:

       − The provisions of the trust account,
       − The beneficiaries' needs,
       − The quality of fund management,
       − The fee structure,
       − Risk diversification, and
       − Rates of return.

    c. Determine whether the trust department conducts periodic reviews of the ongoing prudence of the investment. Such reviews should cover:

       − The quality of the holdings,
       − The compatibility of investment objectives, and
       − The availability of competing investments, including non-proprietary products, which might better meet the fiduciary account's investment objectives.

Compliance Program

19. Determine how effective the bank's compliance program is by reviewing:

- Responses to the Compliance Program section of the ICQ,
- The independence of compliance personnel,
- Training provided to compliance personnel,
- Automated exception reporting systems, and
- The scope, frequency, and findings of compliance reviews, and responses to findings.

20. Determine whether results of periodic reviews are formally communicated to senior managers independent of the sales function, and whether a follow-up system tracks management responses to noted exceptions.

21. If prior examination findings, compliance reports, a pattern of customer complaints, or routine oversight by bank management identifies the possibility that suitability problems may exist, determine if bank management has conducted a thorough review of all affected accounts and instituted appropriate corrective actions.

Third Party Vendors

22. Determine the effectiveness of the bank's oversight program and whether bank management has discharged its responsibilities under the program.

   a. Review responses under the Third Party Vendor section of the ICQ and the text of the bank's oversight program.

   b. Review the scope and frequency of completed and scheduled oversight reviews and reviews of customer complaints and their resolution.

   c. Review bank management's response to recommendations made during past examinations.

   d. Review the third party vendor agreement and determine:

   – Whether it specifies that such entities will comply with all applicable requirements, including those in the Interagency Statement.

        – How bank management assures itself that third party vendors comply with the terms of the agreement.

    e. Review how bank management determined the adequacy of the steps a third party vendor takes to avoid customer confusion about the nature of the product and the bank's role in the sales process.

    f. Determine whether bank management understands and agrees with the way the third party vendor selects products.

23. After making a judgment about the effectiveness of the oversight of third party vendor sales, complete any other examination procedures that appear appropriate.

Summary

24. Determine if bank management has demonstrated by its actions whether it believes customers' interests are critical to all aspects of its nondeposit investment product sales programs.

25. Discuss significant findings with the EIC and bank management and prepare written comments.

Retail Nondeposit Investment Sales (Section 413)   Internal Control Questionnaire

Program Management

1. Has the bank's board of directors adopted a program management statement that addresses:

    - The features of the sales program?
    - The associated risks?
    - The roles of bank employees?
    - The roles of third party entities?

2. Do the bank's policies address the following issues:

    - Program objectives?
    - Strategies to be employed to achieve objectives?
    - Supervision of personnel involved in nondeposit investment sales programs?
    - Supervisory responsibilities of third party vendors who are selling on bank premises?
    - Selection of the products the bank will sell?
    - Permissible uses of bank customer information?
    - Communications with customers?
    - The setting and circumstances of nondeposit product sales?
    - Disclosures and advertising?
    - Suitability of recommendations?
    - Employee qualifications and training?
    - Employee compensation systems?
    - A compliance program?

3. Do written supervisory procedures assign a manager the responsibility for:

- Reviewing and authorizing each sale?
- Accepting each new account?
- Reviewing and authorizing all sales or account-related correspondence with customers?
- Reviewing and authorizing all advertising and promotional materials prior to use?

4. Does the bank use written job descriptions to assign management responsibilities?

5. Do policies and procedures for personnel who are not directly involved in nondeposit investment product sales detail what the employees may say and not say about investment products?

Product Selection

6. Does the bank select the products to be offered?

7. If so, does the selection process make use of predetermined criteria that consider the customers' needs?

8. Does a qualified committee or an analyst who is independent of the sales function make the product selections?

9. If the bank uses outside consultants to help select products, does bank management determine if the consultant receives compensation from product issuers or wholesalers?

10. If the product selection analysis is performed by another party, such as a clearing broker or third party vendor, does bank management understand and agree with the analysis method?

11. Does the bank conduct continuing reviews of product offerings to assure that they remain acceptable and are such reviews done at least annually?

12. Does bank management consider, as part of the selection process, the product issuer's contingency plans for dealing with unusual surges in redemptions?

13. Are these contingency plans based on various market scenarios?

14. Do the contingency plans include:

   • Emergency staffing?
   • Additional communications capabilities?
   • Enhanced operational support?

15. Does the analysis of fixed and variable rate annuities include a determination of the credit quality of the issuing insurance company?

16. Does the analysis of fixed and variable rate annuities include determining whether the issuing insurance company can sell or simply transfer the annuity contract to another insurance company?

Use of Customer Information

17. Do written policies concerning the use of information about bank customers address:

   • The minimum standards or criteria for identifying a customer for solicitation?
   • Acceptable calling times?
   • The number of times a customer may be called?
   • The steps to be taken to avoid confusing depositors about the nature of the products being offered?

Setting and Circumstances of Nondeposit Sales

18. Has a bank officer been assigned responsibility for reviewing all current and planned nondeposit investment sales locations to determine whether appropriate measures are in place to minimize customer confusion?

19. Are nondeposit investment products sold only at locations distinct from where deposits are accepted?

20. Are sales locations distinguished by use of:

- Separate desks?
- Distinguishing partitions, railings, or planters?
- Signs?

21. If personnel both accept deposits and sell nondeposit investment products, do operating procedures address safeguards to prevent possible customer confusion?

22. Are the people who sell nondeposit investment products distinguished from people who accept deposits by such means as:

- Name tags or badges?
- Business cards?

23. Do operating procedures prohibit tellers from offering investment advice, making sales recommendations, or discussing the merits of any nondeposit investment product with customers?

24. Does the bank offer nondeposit investment products with product names that are not:

- Identical to the bank's name?
- Similar to a deposit product?
  (Example: XYZ Money Market Fund vs. XYZ Money Market Account.)

25. Does the bank avoid using the words "insured," "bank," or "national" in product names?

Disclosures and Advertising

26. Has bank management designated an officer to be responsible for ensuring that bank-prepared investment advertisements and advertisements prepared by any other party are accurate and include all required disclosures?

27. Is a signed statement acknowledging disclosures obtained from each customer at the time that a retail nondeposit investment account is opened?

28. For accounts established prior to the issuance of the Interagency Statement, are procedures in place to ensure that such a signed statement is obtained prior to, or at the time of, the next transaction?

29. Is there a tracking system designed to monitor and obtain missing acknowledgments?

30. Are all salespeople provided written disclosure guidelines for oral presentations?

31. Do the guidelines for oral presentations clearly direct the speaker to:

    • State the required disclosures?
    • Clarify the bank's role in the sales process?

32. If ratings are used in promoting certain products, does bank policy indicate whether the bank will disclose ratings changes?

33. If so, does policy indicate how such disclosures will occur?

34. If the bank is selling annuities that can be transferred to another obligor, is this possibility disclosed to prospective customers?

Suitability

35. Has a bank officer been assigned responsibility for implementing and monitoring the suitability system?

36. Are systems in place to ensure that any salespeople involved in bank-related sales obtain sufficient information from customers to enable them to make a judgment about the suitability of recommendations for particular customers?

37. Do suitability inquiries include information concerning the customer's:

    • Financial and tax status?
    • Investment objectives?

- Other information such as date of birth, employment, net worth (net of residential real estate), income, current investments, or risk tolerance?

38. Are customer responses to suitability inquiries documented on a standard form or any other method that permits ready review?

39. Is there a tracking system designed to monitor and obtain missing suitability information?

40. Are new accounts reviewed and formally accepted by a manager before the first transfer is finalized?

41. Does the new account acceptance process include a review of the suitability inquiry and customer responses?

42. Is each sale approved in writing by a designated manager?

43. Are breakpoints considered in both the initial recommendation and in the review of the suitability of those recommendations?

44. Is suitability information for active accounts updated periodically?

45. If the bank uses software programs to assist salespersons in making suitability judgments, does the program:

- Weight bank proprietary products and bank deposits similarly to other products?
- Consider breakpoints?

46. If a software program is not used, has management identified which products meet certain investment objectives, or has management generally categorized products as suitable for either unsophisticated, sophisticated, or risk-averse customers?

47. Does the bank use suitability guidelines that would limit certain transactions with first time or risk-averse investors, or would require a higher level of approval?

48. Is a bank officer who is independent of the sales force assigned responsibility for reviewing complaints and their resolution?

Qualifications and Training

49. Does the bank's staffing plan consider its nondeposit investment sales program?

50. Does the bank seek to employ dedicated investment specialists and not platform generalists as sales representatives?

51. Does management have written qualification requirements for outside hires of salespeople and sales program managers?

52. Is a system in place to document background inquiries made about new bank sales employees who have previous securities industry experience to check for a possible disciplinary history?

53. Has a bank officer been assigned responsibility for ensuring that adequate training is provided to bank staff?

54. Does the bank have a formal training program for individuals who:

- Make customer referrals for nondeposit products?
- Are engaged in retail sales of nondeposit investment products?
- Are responsible for supervising people who make referrals and/or who engage in selling?

55. Is this training offered as part of:

- Initial training?
- Continuing training?

56. Is there a training manual showing the objectives of each initial and subsequent training session?

57. Have lesson plans been developed for in-house programs?

58. Are tellers trained:

- To not accept orders or sell nondeposit investment products?
- To avoid offering investment advice?
- To not make recommendations?
- To not discuss the merits of any securities with customers?

59. Does the bank provide training that addresses suitability issues?

60. Does suitability training specifically address customer protection issues associated with the most vulnerable classes of investors who may actually prefer the "no investment risk" aspect of insured bank deposits?

61. Is product training provided to:

- Compliance staff?
- Audit staff?

62. Does the bank have a formal plan to meet future retail nondeposit investment product sales training needs?

Compensation

63. Are compensation systems set up to avoid paying the same people incentive compensation for the sale of nondeposit investment products when no incentives are paid for renewing certificates of deposit?

64. Do supervisory policies control incentive compensation increases associated with sales contests or the introduction of new products?

65. Are referral programs designed so that employees, including tellers, may receive a one-time nominal fee of a fixed dollar amount for each customer referred, without regard for whether the sale is made?

66. Do policies prohibit tellers from participating in contests or other promotional programs in which prizes are based on successful sales to customers referred?

67. Do policies and procedures preclude incentive compensation based on

the profitability of individual trades by, or accounts subject to the review of, bank employees who:

- Review and approve individual sales?
- Accept new accounts?
- Review established customer accounts?

68. Do policies and procedures preclude payment of incentive compensation to department auditors or compliance personnel?

69. Does the management structure preclude control, audit or compliance personnel from reporting to managers whose compensation is based on profits from nondeposit investment products sales?

70. Does the compensation program reduce remuneration to sales program managers whose accounts show:

- Missing documents?
- Unreported customer complaints?
- Reversed or "bad" sales?
- Compliance problems?

Compliance Program

71. Do audit or compliance personnel:

- Determine the scope and frequency of their own nondeposit investment sales program reviews?
- Report their findings directly to the board of directors or an appropriate committee of the board?
- Have their performance evaluated by persons independent of the investment product sales function?
- Receive compensation that in no way is connected to the success of investment product sales?
- Receive training in products and customer protection issues?
- Keep abreast of emerging developments in banking and securities laws and regulations through ongoing training?

72. Does the bank's written compliance program call for periodic reviews to determine compliance with policies, procedures, applicable laws and regulations, and the Interagency Statement? Do those reviews cover:

- Customer complaints and their resolution?
- Customer correspondence?
- Transactions with employees and directors or their business interests?
- All advertising and promotional materials?
- Scripts or written guidelines for oral presentations?
- Training materials?
- Regular and frequent reviews of active customer accounts?
- Customer responses to suitability inquiries and a periodic comparison of those responses to the type and volume of account activity, with the goal of determining whether the activity in an account is appropriate?

73. Does the compliance program call for compliance personnel to perform continuing reviews of:

- Changes in the system for reporting customer complaints and resolutions?
- Changes in previously approved standard correspondence with customers?
- New advertising and promotional materials prior to use?
- Changes in existing training programs or new training programs?
- Changes in incentive compensation systems?
- New products under development?

74. Does the timing, scope, and frequency of compliance reviews consider factors such as:

- Changes or differences in incentive compensation paid on different or new products?
- Sales or referral contests?
- Patterns of sales for specific, especially new, products?
- Patterns of sales to customers who have been identified as risk-averse investors?

- New salespeople?
- Customer complaints?

75. Does the bank have a system for ensuring that all complaints (written and oral) receive bank management's attention?

76. Is that system periodically tested by internal audit to determine whether bank management receives notice of all complaints?

77. Does the bank use automated exception reporting systems to flag potential compliance problems?

78. Do reports list:

- Sales by product?
- Significant or unusual (for the customer) individual sales?
- Sales of products the bank considers more volatile to customers whose suitability inquiry responses indicate an aversion to risk?
- Customer complaints by product, salesperson, and reason, so that patterns can be discerned?
- Unusual performance by salespersons, e.g., high or low volume or single product sales?
- Significant volumes of annuity or mutual fund redemptions after short holding periods?

79. Do reports provide adequate information to conduct specific suitability reviews for customers such as:

- Risk-averse investors?
- First-time investors?
- Customers with other narrow investment objectives?

80. Does the bank employ "testers" who pose as prospective customers and test the sales presentations for adherence to customer protection standards?

81. Has the bank instituted a follow-up contact program to verify whether customers understand their investment transactions?

82. Do inquiries in the follow-up contact program include discussion of the customer's:

- Understanding of what he or she has purchased?
- Understanding of the investment risks and the absence of deposit insurance coverage?
- Initial responses to the salesperson's suitability inquiry?
- Understanding of fees?
- Problems or complaints?
- Understanding of the bank's role in the transaction?

83. If the bank operates a follow-up contact program, are records of customers' responses maintained?

Third Party Vendors

84. Has a bank officer been assigned responsibility for ensuring that the bank adequately monitors the effectiveness of customer protection systems?

85. Has the bank developed a written oversight program to monitor the activities of outside vendors operating bank-related sales programs?

86. Does the governing agreement with third party vendors include provisions regarding:

- Training for bank employees?
- Methods of implementing the customer protection standards contained in the bank's policy?
- Permission for the OCC and the bank to have access to appropriate records involved in bank-related sales?
- The scope and frequency of reports to be furnished?

87. Do reports furnished by third party vendors include:

- A list of all new account openings and initial trades?
- A list of significant or unusual (for the customer) individual sales?
- A list of all written and oral customer complaints and their

resolution?

- Sales reports by product, salesperson, and location?
- Internal compliance reviews of accounts originated at the bank?
- Copies of reports furnished to the third party vendor by their regulator?

88. Are reports furnished by a third party vendor:

   - Prepared by someone independent of the vendor's sales force?
   - Timely and sufficiently detailed?

89. Does bank management have procedures in place to avoid reliance on third party audit and control systems if the vendor's control personnel receive transaction-base incentive compensation?

90. If the product selection analysis is performed by another party, such as a clearing broker or third party vendor, does bank management understand and agree with the analysis method?

91. If customer information is provided to the third party vendor, has a legal opinion concerning the bank's authority to share customer information with third parties been obtained?

92. Has a bank officer been assigned responsibility for ensuring that adequate training is provided to bank staff, and for reviewing the hiring and training practices of any third party vendor?